CONTENTS

1. **About This Book**

2. **Forms Needed for Your Green Card Application**

    Forms-I-130 and I-130A or Petition for Alien Relative and Supplemental Information
    Form I-485 Application to Register Permanent Residence
    Form G-28 Attorney Representation
    Form G-1145 E-notification
    Form I-944 Declaration of Self-Sufficiency
    Form I-693 or Medical Examination Form
    Form I-765 or Employment Authorization Form
    Form I-131 or Application for Travel Document
    Form I-864, Affidavit of Support

3. **Typical Interview Questions**

    General advice

    Interview Questions

    Personal Information Questions
    The history of your relationship and marriage typical questions
    Questions about your parents, children, relatives, friends, and prior spouses
    Questions about your home, car, home address history, and neighborhood
    Questions about your spouse's activities and hobbies
    A note on race, religion, and age differences
    Questions about your taxes, employment, and education
    Bringing an attorney to the green card interview
    Bringing an interpreter to the green card interview
    What can be done if your immigration application is pending for a long time?

4. **Supporting Documents**

    General Types of Documents for Form I-130 and Form I-495
    Documents to prove US Citizenship or permanent residence
    Documents needed to prove family relations and financial ties
    Possible issues to avoid
    Work Permit and Travel Document

1. About this book

The goal of this book is to demystify the marriage-based green card interview and prepare couples for possible interview questions and required supporting documents to establish that the marriage is valid. In this book, we provide many sample questions that you are likely to be asked during the interview and offer a detailed review of the supporting documents that you must provide to support your application.

The author of this book is a practicing attorney who specializes in, among other areas, immigration law and has hands-on experience in negotiating family-based immigration. The author is a graduate from of the Touro College Jacob D. Fuchsberg Law Center in Central Islip, NY. Even before becoming an attorney, the author worked as an interpreter in an immigration law office. He also assisted his friends and relatives in preparing their green card applications. The author is not affiliated with any immigration agency and this book represents his personal legal experiences and opinions.

The reader of this book should keep in mind that the immigration law is very fluid and the United States Citizenship and Immigration Services (USCIS) changes its forms and procedures frequently. Thus, people preparing to file a marriage-based green card application should always consult the latest immigration forms and instructions for these forms on the USCIS website or contact an immigration attorney for professional advice.

As this book finds its readers, the author is contemplating work a second edition in the future and the possible addition of new chapters to address the complexity immigration laws and procedures. The readers are welcome to comment on the book and share their own stories about the green card application and interview process. The author can be reached via his website and his email at www.istominlaw.com and istominesq@gmail.com.

Good luck with your green card interview!
Copyright © 2020 by Vladimir Istomin, Esq.

2. Forms needed for your green card application

In this short introductory chapter, I list the forms needed for the green card application to provide a full picture of the entire application process. These forms and the instructions for these forms are available free of charge on the immigration website, www.uscis.gov. Moreover, please note that the immigration service frequently makes changes to the forms and may add additional forms. The forms described here represent the way the forms were listed at the time this book was written.

Forms-I-130 and I-130A Petition for Alien Relative and Supplemental Information

These are the initial forms that the spouse who is the US citizen or green card holder must file files on behalf of her foreign spouse. These forms ask you to provide basic biographic and employment information. In theory, you can just file these forms, wait until they are approved, and then file the rest of the forms, or else you can file all of the forms separately. Filing the Form-130 separately and waiting for approval before filing the rest of the application, however, will double your waiting time for the interview. There is no point in filing the forms separately, unless you are short on money and cannot afford to pay all of the immigration fees at once, or you need time to obtain additional documents for other forms.

Form I-485 Application to Register Permanent Residence

This form asks you to provide more detailed biographic information about the spouse seeking the green card, the address history, and previous marriages, and so on. It also has a long list of yes or no questions as to whether the applicant was engaged in any illegal activities.

Form G-28 Attorney Representation

If you are represented by an attorney, your attorney has to file this form and the clients need to sign it.

Form G-1145 E-notification

This form is an optional form, filed to request notification via email about the status of your application. Please note that you can also submit your application electronically. In the past, there were some issues reported concerning the electronic upload of supporting documents to the USCIS website. My recommendation is to file your application the old fashioned way, via certified mail with a return receipt and you should keep a copy of everything that was mailed to the USCIS. Further, please note that you may give the USCIS a PO Box address for all correspondence. If you change your address while your application is still pending, you must notify the USCIS about your new address by filing a Form AR-11 by mail or on-line.

Form I-944 Declaration of Self-Sufficiency

This is a new form that was recently added by the USCIS. The purpose of this form is to establish that the applicant is self-sufficient financially and will not become a public burden. In short, the applicant must provide information about his household income, liabilities, medical insurance, past public benefits, education, and special vocational skills. We will discuss the supporting documents for this form in the chapter about the supporting documents.

Form I-693 or Medical Examination Form

The USCIS requires the green card applicant to have a medical examination form and have proper vaccination. The USCIS maintains a list of approved doctors on its website and you cannot ask your regular doctor to complete this form. However, the USCIS doctor will accept a medical vaccination note from your regular doctor, so you do not have to have the vaccines administered twice. The current website link for the list of the USCIS approved doctors is https://my.uscis.gov/findadoctor. This form is valid for two years. If your interview is delayed for more than two years, which is possible, given the long interview delays characteristic of the current situation, you are required to provide a new form.

Form I-765 Employment Authorization Form

You must file this form to be authorized to work in the USA. Once approved, the USCIS will mail you an employment authorization ID. The employment authorization is usually issued in about six months or so and before you are issued the actual green card, so you can work legally while your green card is still pending. We will discuss the employment authorization form in detail in the chapter about the supporting documents.

Form I-131 Application for Travel Document

This is an optional form that the applicant can file that, in theory, allows the applicant to travel abroad while waiting for the green card to be approved. The good news is that the USCIS fee is waived if you file this form together with your initial application. The bad news is that this document is intended for emergency travel only, such as if your close relative is terminally ill abroad. You need to provide evidence that you, indeed, have an emergency abroad such as, for example, medical records. Further, the USCIS maintains that the agency has broad discretion to refuse the holder of the travel document reentry into the USA.

Form I-864 Affidavit of Support

This form is usually filed by the spouse who is a US citizen or the green card holder, and it allows the spouse to pledge to provide the financial support the immigrant spouse and to ensure that the immigrant spouse will not become a public burden. This form can also be completed by any other individual, such as friend or a relative, who is willing to support the applicant and who has a higher income or significant assets, in case the US citizen spouse has a low income. Certain applicants are exempt from filing this form, such as applicants who have worked in the USA and earned 40 Social Security credits or applicants filing under the battered spouse provision.

3. Typical Interview Questions

Clients preparing for a marriage-based green card interview often ask what kinds of questions the interviewing officer will ask them. This chapter is intended to give you an idea of which questions to expect during the interview. Preparing for the interview in advance will give you an advantage and make you more comfortable and **confident** during the questions.

Keep in mind that the main goal of the interview is to determine whether your marriage is legitimate and was not arranged. The interview is the most stressful part of the green card application process. However, if you prepare for the interview and know what to expect, you should be able to avoid such stress, master the answers, and pass the interview.

General advice

You should practice for the interview by holding an at-home mock interview in which one spouse pretends to be an interviewing officer and asks the other spouse questions.

Alternatively, one of your friends could act as an interviewer. Have a copy of your file with you during the interview. It is all right to tell the interviewing officer that you do not remember a particular date (for example, when you moved from a particular address) and look it up in your file.

Be prepared for the interviewing officer to be hostile and intimidating. Remain calm, **and** answer the questions to the best of your ability or memory. Some couples expect officers to be friendly, but they are often aggressive and imposing.

Usually, both spouses are present in the same room during the interview, but questions are addressed to one spouse at a time, and the other cannot answer or help with the answers. If the interviewing officer suspects fraud, the interview could be conducted separately.

You should therefore prepare for the possibility that the interview will be conducted separately and that both spouses' answers will be compared later. In real life, the answers to some questions could be ambiguous and not straightforward. However, the interviewing officer will expect a quick and direct answer from you.

For example, imagine that a couple met on a dating website, but they told all their friends that they met on a vacation in Mexico because this sounded more romantic. In this situation, when asked where they spouse their spouse, the might delay answering the while considering whether to say that they met on the Internet or in Mexico. However, an officer could interpret such a delay in answering a simple question as indicating potential fraud. Thus, you should discuss with your spouse all potentially ambiguous answers, and decide on the answer beforehand. Then, when asked, answer the question quickly and confidentially.

In addition, consider the following advice on how to dress for the interview and how to behave during the interview. You should dress respectfully, but not overdress, consider wearing business-casual clothing. Dress as though this is your first day at a new job in an office environment. In addition, do not use a strong perfume with an unusual smell.

While waiting for the interview in the waiting area, you should sit next to each other, and you should consider exhibiting some signs of affection, such as putting a hand on your spouse. The interviewing officer might be observing you in the waiting area, so if you sit apart and pay no attention to each other, this could arouse a suspicion that your relationship is not genuine.

From my observation, it is not a good idea to try to become familiar with the officer and joke around or be sarcastic with them. After all, the officer's goal is to establish whether your marriage is real. If you make a funny comment, an officer might interpret it as a factual statement and count it against you.

You should answer the questions you are asked, but if you volunteer more information than the officer requests, you should also be prepared to answer some follow-up questions on this topic. You could decline to answer if you find it offensive, or you could tell the officer that you do not remember a particular date or fact, but you cannot decline too many questions this way. **Just be polite and calm**. You should also try to answer the questions quickly because if you delay, the interviewing officer could get the impression that you are making up an answer.

The interviewing officer is not your friend; such a person is neutral at best. In your particular situation, you could encounter an antagonistic officer who does not like you for one reason or another or who is just not in a good mood on this particular day. Still, the officer must follow certain guidelines. If you answer all questions correctly and have good supporting evidence, your application must be approved.

Interview Questions

The following are typical questions a couple can expect to encounter during their interview.

Personal Information Questions

The interview usually starts with basic informational questions about facts such as your name, address, date and place of birth, and contact information. Spouses are interviewed together, and the interview usually lasts about 30 minutes. However, if the interviewing officer suspects that your marriage is arranged, you could be placed in separate rooms. In such cases, the spouses are questioned separately, and their answers compared later. If the spouses' answers do not match, the couple fails the interview. Therefore, it is important to practice at home, and it is a good idea to have two copies of your application and supporting documents.

The interviewer could also ask questions about your prior marriages and any other names you have used. You should have valid forms of identifications, such as a U.S. passport for the spouse who is a U.S. citizen (or green card if you are a green card holder) and a foreign passport for the spouse who is applying for the green card. The foreign passport should be valid and not expired. The officer may ask whether your U.S. visa was ever denied and whether you visited the U.S. previously. If you answer yes, you might be asked what type of visa you had, and whether you were a citizen of any other country in the past.

Double-check your passport before going the interview as you might accidently grab your old, expired passport or the passport of a relative living in your household. I have seen these types of situations. You should also have your original social security cards, original employment authorization card, original birth certificates, and original citizenship certificate if you have one.

The officer might also ask whether you have applied for a green card before and, if so what the result of your application was. If a spouse who is a U.S. citizen gained their citizenship via an immigration application, the officer may ask about the details of how this spouse obtained U.S. citizenship and the date and manner in which you entered the United Sates.

It is important to note that persons who entered the United States illegally cannot obtain a green card via marriage to a U.S. citizen or green card holder. However, if you simply overstayed your visa, you usually remain eligible for a green card. There are some exceptions however, as some educational grants may require the recipient to return to their country of origin. Still, even these exceptions can be appealed.

Please also note that if your immigrant spouse worked in the United States illegally, this is usually not an immigration bar for the green card. However, working illegally could be a bar for most other types of immigrants. Only immediate relatives such as spouses, minor children, and parents are permitted this waiver.

In addition, the spouse who is applying for the green card must submit a copy of their medical examination with your initial application. The examination is good for two years. Your regular doctor may not provide you with the medical examination form. Instead, the USCIS maintains a list of approved doctors on its website for examination purposes. The examination form is given to you in a sealed envelope. The interviewing officer may also ask you some follow-up questions about your medical examination and your health issues.

The history of your relationship and marriage typical questions

- How and where did you meet your spouse?

- Where was your first date?

- How long did you have a relationship before you decided to get married?

- Who proposed?

- How and when the marriage proposal take place?

- When and where did you meet each other's parents?

- Did your parents approve of your relationship?

- When and where your marriage ceremony or wedding took place, and who attended?

- Did you go to a particular restaurant for the wedding?

- Which friends and relatives did you invite?

- Did you go on a honeymoon trip after the wedding?

Be prepared to explain the related details and circumstances. If you have some pictures or other evidence connected to these events, bring them with you to show the officer.

You absolutely must know your spouse's important dates such as birthday, and be prepared to give details on how you celebrated this birthday or a recent holiday and what kind of gifts you gave each other. How do you usually celebrate a particular holiday? If you were not together for an important holiday, this is a warning sign for an interviewing officer, so you must have a good explanation.

Wedding ring. Even if you do not like wearing a wedding ring, you should wear one the interview. In fact, you should start wearing it prior to the interview, so there is a mark on your finger.

Some questions about your relationship could include questions about your joint activities. For example, which movie did you see together last? Where did you go for your last vacation? Have pictures from your last vacation and other joint activities.

Questions about your intimate life are rare, but an interviewing officer could questions such as the following:

- What is the color of your wife's underwear today?
- Which side of the bed does your spouse sleep on?
- Do you use any contraceptives?
- What kind of clothing does your spouse wear to bed?
- Do you have an alarm clock, if so, what color is it?
- What did you do last night?
- When was the last time you had sex?
- What color is your bed frame, and what size is your mattress?
- Do you have a night light in your bedroom?

Questions about your parents, children, relatives, friends, and prior spouses

Expect a few questions related to your spouse's parents, relatives, friends, and any children from a prior marriage. You should also know names, birthdays, occupations, and other general information about people related to your spouse.

For, example, an interviewing officer might ask if your spouse has any brothers and sisters, as well as where they live, what kind of work they do, and when you saw them last. N officer might also ask who your spouse's best friend is.

There could also be questions about your spouse's parents, such as where they reside, when they were born, and whether they have died. In the last case, you may also be asked where and when they passed away. You might also have to answer questions about your prior spouses, such as when and where you were married to and divorced from them. You are required to submit copies of your prior marriage and divorce certificates with your initial green card applications. You should bring the original prior marriage and divorce certificates to the interview.

If your spouse has children from a previous marriage, you are expected to have detailed information about them, such as what school or daycare the child attends, the names of their teachers, the child's favorite activities, the name of the babysitter, the child's favorite toy, and the child's favorite food.

The good news is that if you have a child or children together, you are quite likely to pass the interview. It is hard to imagine that an interviewing officer would suspect fraud if a married couple has children. Still, bring the pictures of your children and point out to the interviewing officer that you have children together. Other questions about children may include when and where they were born. If a child is not living with you, the officer may ask where this child resides. If the wife is pregnant, this is also a considerable factor in your favor that indicates the marriage is real. Bring a doctor's note indicating that the wife is pregnant and give it to the interviewing officer.

Questions about your home, car, home address history, and neighborhood

Questions of this type are meant to establish that the spouses live together. For example, the interviewing officer could ask the following:

- What color is the laundry bin in your house?
- What is the color of the curtains in the bedroom?
- How is the furniture arranged in your living room?
- What color are the appliances in your kitchen?
- Where are the television and the computer in your house?
- At which supermarket do you shop for groceries?
- Who usually does the grocery shopping?
- Where is your nearest post office?
- What is your favorite restaurant in your neighborhood?
- What is your favorite park in your neighborhood?
- What church or other religious institution do you attend in your neighborhood?

- What car do you drive?
- Do you have a pet in your household, and if so, what is its name?
- What is your typical breakfast?
- What are the names of your utility company, cable company, and phone company?
- What is your favorite television channel or show?
- What brands of shampoo, laundry detergent, and toothpaste do you use?
- Where do you keep medications in your house?
- If you live in a single-family home, on what day of the week is your garbage is collected?
- Do you have a mortgage for your house, and if so, how much is it for, and with which bank?

The interviewing officer is almost certain to ask you about your address history, as well as when you moved in and out at a particular address. The officer has all of this information in front of him in your immigration application. As the immigration application takes a long time, by the time you are called for the interview, you might not remember the exact dates and addresses of your prior housing, especially if you have moved around a few times. The interviewing officer can also ask you about your last address abroad.

Therefore, try to refresh your memory before the interview and review your address history from a copy of your application. In addition, have a copy of your application in front of you so you can double-check the exact date. If you look up this information from your application during the interview, this should still count as the correct answer. Just say something like "Sorry, I don't remember the exact date. I think it was during the summer, but let me double-check. Oh, no, it was in March." Bingo! This is a checkmark in your favor, and you just scored a point.

Questions about your spouse's activities and hobbies

You could be asked questions such as these:

- What is your spouse's favorite color?
- What is your spouse's favorite perfume?
- Who takes care of the family finances?
- What kind of music does your spouse like?
- Which radio station does your spouse prefer?
- Which social events have you attended together recently?
- How often do you eat out?
- How much money does your spouse make, and what is his or her place of employment?

Bring pictures from social events, family activities, sports events you have attended, or outings to a park. There could also be questions about your spouse's hobbies, employment, or character, such as these:

- Where does your spouse work?
- At What time do they go to work?
- Who are your spouse's friends?
- What kind of food do you cook?

Moreover, there could be questions about your daily routines:

- Who wakes up first and at what time do they wake up?
- On which side of the bed does your spouse sleep?
- What medications does your spouse take?

A note on race, religion, and age differences

Although the interviewing officer cannot deny your green card application if your spouse is of a deferent race, ethnicity, or religion, or if there is a large age difference between you, such differences might cause the interviewing officer to review your marriage with more scrutiny compared to a couple whose members share an ethnicity, religion, and age range. Just be prepared for extra scrutiny in this type of situation.

Questions about your taxes, employment, and education

When you submit your green card application, the immigration service requires you to submit a copy of your tax transcript. This is not a copy of your tax return, but a document issued by the IRS at your request. You can obtain it by calling the IRS or by submitting a request on the IRS website.

For the interview, you should bring a copy of your tax transcript and a copy of your tax return, as well as all W-2s and similar income forms. The interviewing officer can ask you to see a copy of your tax return and W-2s. There are two main purposes for requiring your tax return. The first is to establish that a financial entanglement exists between the spouses. For this reason, you should always file your tax returns jointly with your spouse because filing separately constitutes a warning sign on your application and may suggest to the interviewing officer that your marriage is arranged. If you filed your taxes separately, you should have a good explanation for why you did so.

If you must file your taxes separately for economic reasons, consider filing a tax extension instead. If you already filed your taxes separately, you could re-file your taxes jointly as the IRS allows you to re-file your taxes for up to three years back. However, be aware that processing your modified tax returns could take a couple of months.

The second reason an interviewing officer might want to see your taxes is to confirm that you have sufficient income and will not be an economic burden for the state. You were already required to submit your income and tax information with your green card information. If you were called for the interview, the immigration office has already checked your income, and you qualify for the green card based on your income. However, at the interview, the interviewing officer will double-check your income qualifications.

This is the income qualification table at the time this book was written. However, the immigration office changes the income requirements frequently, so if your income is on the borderline you should check the income requirement on the internet before submitting your immigration application.

Sponsor's Household Size	100% of HHS Poverty Guidelines*	125% of HHS Poverty Guidelines*
	For sponsors on active duty in the U.S. armed forces who are petitioning for their spouse or child	*For all other sponsors*
2	$17,240	$21,550
3	$21,720	$27,150

Sponsor's Household Size	100% of HHS Poverty Guidelines*	125% of HHS Poverty Guidelines*
4	$26,200	$32,750
5	$30,680	$38,350
6	$35,160	$43,950
7	$39,640	$49,550
8	$44,120	$55,150
	Add $4,480 for each additional person	**Add $5,600 for each additional person**

If you do not meet the income requirements, your application will be rejected. However, you can ask a friend or relative with high income or considerable assets to act as a sponsor on your behalf. In addition, if your income is low, but you have financial assets such as bank accounts, real estate, and similar assets, you may still qualify for the immigration income threshold.

Please also note that the immigration office counts your adjusted income, not your gross income. Your adjusted income is your income after all your deductions.

It is advisable, although it is not required, to have a tax transcript, tax returns, and W-2 forms for the last three years. This way, you can establish that you are a hard-working individual who will not become a public burden in the future.

The interviewing officer is also likely to ask about your present and past jobs. All your jobs are listed on your application. If you changed jobs and do not remember when you started a particular job, you could look this up on a copy of your application during the interview. You should also attach a copy of your employment verification letter and copies of your most recent paystubs to your immigration application, and you should bring copies of these documents to the interview.

The interviewing officer may ask whether you have filed an affidavit of financial support for anyone else in the past and whether you have anyone else living in your household. If you have any financial assets such as real estate, bank or brokerage accounts, and cars, bring titles and statements to demonstrate that you own these assets.

The officer also may ask you about your educational history, such as whether and when you graduated from the high school and college. It is a good idea to bring a copy of your resume to the interview so you have your complete educational and employment history in front of you.

Bringing an attorney to the green card interview

You can also hire an attorney to accompany you to the interview. The attorney might provide you with a much-needed moral and legal support during the interview and could assist you later with filing an appeal and contacting the immigration services if your application is denied. Moreover, in the presence of the attorney, the interviewing officer should be less inclined to use any intimidation-based tactics because the attorney could always intervene on your behalf. The presence of an attorney could be a game-changing factor during the interview.

Bringing an interpreter to the green card interview

Some USCIS officers have interpreters available during the interview, but you are allowed to bring your own interpreter. The interpreter does not have to be a professional interpreter, but they must be a U.S. citizen or green card holder, and they must bring their U.S. passport or green card to the interview.

One spouse is not allowed to interpret for the other or to correct the other spouse's answers. If one of the spouses has limited English ability, it is a good idea to bring your own interpreter because the spouse with limited English ability may misunderstand a question and answer it incorrectly. You and the interpreter must also file a USCIS form G-1256 to have an interpreter present during the interview.

What can be done if your immigration application is pending for a long time?

The USCIS takes a long time to process immigration applications, so you might have to wait to receive a reply. You should submit your application via a certified mail with a return receipt, which can serve as proof that you submitted your application if it becomes lost. You can check the status of your application on the immigration office website, https://egov.uscis.gov/casestatus/landing.do. You can submit an online inquiry about your case on the USCIS website. You can also call the USCIS to ask whether they received your application and what is the status of your case is. In addition, you could schedule an in-person appointment on the USCIS website. Try a few offices in your area, as some are busier than others.

4. Supporting documents

In this chapter, I discuss the supporting documents needed for a successful marriage-based green card application. There are three groups of documents that an applicant must present.

The first group consists of general types of documents, such as birth certificates, marriage certificates, and divorce certificates. The purpose of these documents is to prove your identity, as well as prove that you are the person you claim to be and that your marriage is a valid one, in the sense that this is your first marriage or that any previous marriages have been properly terminated.

The second group of documents consist of are financial, employment, and educational records, which serve to establish that you are in good financial shape and unlikely to become a public burden in the future. If the applicant or his or her spouse previously used some public benefits, this will not bar the application completely, but it must be explained. Moreover, unemployment benefits are not counted against you, so you need not worry if you have previously collected unemployment benefits.

The third group of documents consists of documents to prove family relationships, as well as comingling of finances and other resources. This group of documents is, by far, the most important and many applicants fail to present the necessary evidence in this context. If you fail to establish family relationship and comingling of finances, your application will be denied. The interviewing officer may overlook a few minor discrepancies in the biographic information and that a spouse received some public assistance in the past, but a lack of documents to establish your family ties is pretty much a deal-breaker.

General types of documents **for Form I-130 and Form I-495**

Documents to prove US Citizenship or permanent residence

If you are a spouse who is a U.S. citizen, you are required to submit a copy of your U.S. passport (or green card or foreign passport with a stamp of permanent residence, if you are a green card holder) with your application and you must bring the original U.S. passport to the interview. Alternatively, you can submit a copy of your U.S. citizenship certificate, naturalization certificate, U.S. birth certificate, or Consular Report of Birth Abroad to establish your U.S. citizenship. If you bring a U.S. passport, be sure that it is not expired.

Foreign passport. If you are a spouse who is a foreign citizen, you are required to submit copies of the passport that you used upon your arrival in the USA, your U.S. visa, and the front and back of your I-94 form. You should also submit a copy of your current foreign passport if is a different from one you used to enter the country. For the interview, bring your old and new foreign passports if you still have both. A word about submitting a copy of your passport and other documents. You should use clear and legitimate copies, made on a copy machine or a scanner, on a white background, and do not submit copies rendered as pictures on your phone which may produce a distorted image. A poor copy of this class of documents may cause a significant delay in your application.

Birth certificates, marriage certificates, divorce certificates, death certificate of a former spouse, certificate of marriage annulment, and court certificate of a name change

You should submit all of these documents with your initial application. If the original documents are in a foreign language, you must submit translations. The good news is that you can translate the documents yourself; you need only to write at the bottom of the document that the translation is a true and accurate translation of the original document, along with your notarized signature.

Try to translate these documents word by word stick as closely as possible to the original documents; this includes translating what is written on the seal of the document, if the document has an official seal. Do not merely give a summary of the document in your translation because the USCIS may reject such a translation. Technically, you should bring all the original birth certificates, marriage certificates, and divorce certificates, but in my experience, the interviewing officer rarely wants to see the originals during the interview, provided that you have submitted good quality copies with the original application.

The reason that the immigration officer will want to see your old marriage certificates and divorce certificates if you were previously married is to confirm that all of your previous marriages were ended legally. If you have a spouse abroad from whom you were never legally divorced or obtained a divorce by some kind of fraud, your current marriage in the USA will be deemed invalid. If you are granted a green card, but it later comes to light that your previous marriage was never legally terminated, your green card will be revoked.

It is a very bad idea to lie to an immigration officer or to forge documents; if you are caught engaged in such acts, your application can be barred permanently and you may be deported. If there is any sort of a typo in one of your documents, it is preferable that you take the time to obtain a corrected document or provide an explanation to the immigration officer. In my experience, even if the original foreign document has a minor typo or correction, it is not a big deal and will not cause a problem with your application.

Optional Documents

If you have any prior arrests or a criminal record, you must submit these records to the USCIS. If you have minor violations on your record, it is likely your application can still be approved, but you should consult an attorney if you have prior arrests. In my experience, even applicants who have somewhat serious violations on their records, such as driving while intoxicated, may be granted green cards. You may be required to attach additional documents to demonstrate that you are reformed, such as documentation of volunteering, participating in public projects, and to provide some good character references from public or religious organizations.

If one of the spouses has ever served in the U.S. military or a military of a foreign country, this spouse should provide the appropriate military records and translations, if the documents are in a foreign language.

Also, if you have ever been the subject of deportation proceedings or had previous or have been charged with any immigration violations, you must provide the appropriate records to the USCIS.

Documents needed to establish that the applicant spouse is not going to become a public burden, and can support himself or herself, or that the other spouse can support his or her spouse or Public Charge Test for Form I-944

There was a relatively recent change in the marriage-based green card application process, when the USCIS introduced a new Form I-944, the declaration of self-sufficiency. In this form, the applicant must provide various kinds of financial information about himself or herself, as well as the members of the household and include the supporting documents. The purpose of this form is to prove that the applicant will be financially self-sufficient and unlikely to become a public burden.

For this form, the USCIS requires you to provide the proof of income for all of the household family income and submit a copy of the IRS transcript from the most recent tax year. It is also helpful, although not required, to attach copies of employment verification letters and recent pay stubs from your company. You should also bring copies of these records to your interview.

Additionally, you are required to list all of your assets and liabilities, and provide supporting documents for these as well. You should only list significant assets and liabilities with a value of at least several hundred dollars. Examples of assets include bank accounts, cars, real estate, and collectible items. For each asset you list, you should attach a supporting document, such as a bank statement, car title, house appraisal, copy of the mortgage, and deed. You should provide a supporting document for each liability as well. An example of an evidence of liability is a mortgage statement for your mortgage loan. The assets and liabilities should be provided for all of the household members.

The USCIS not only wants to know about all of your assets and liabilities, but, also requests that you provide a copy of your credit report from the last 12 months or evidence that you do not have a credit report. The USCIS has an instruction page on its website, detailing how to obtain a credit report. For evidence that you do not have a credit report, you can contact a credit agency; if you receive a return letter or email back indicating that you have no credit file. This would serve as evidence that you do not have a credit file. Additionally, if you make an online inquiry with a credit agency and your file is not found, you can print the internet browser page that stating that there is no credit file in your name.

The USCIS also wants to know if you have ever filed for bankruptcy in the USA or a foreign country and if you have done so, you must to provide details about your bankruptcy filing.

The USCIS also wants to know if you have medical insurance and will request details of your medical insurance coverage, such as when the start and ends dates of the coverage. The best evidence of insurance coverage is an official letter from your medical insurance company, stating the details of your coverage. A copy of your insurance card is not sufficient evidence of coverage. If you do not have insurance, you may obtain a quote for coverage that you plan to obtain in the future and attach it to your application, together with evidence that you have sufficient funds to obtain such coverage.

You should also list in your application all public assistance that you have ever received such as food stamps, public housing, and similar types of public benefits. In my experience, the USCIS does run an independent investigation on the applicant's public benefits, at least for some applicants, so it is not a good idea to misrepresent yourself by claiming that you have never obtained public benefits, if you received such benefits in the past. Having received occasional public benefits is not necessarily a bar to your application, but rather another factor among many. However, if you have continuously received multiple public benefits over a long period, your application may be in trouble. Moreover, the USCIS does not count unemployment benefits against you.

The USCIS also requires you to provide information and supporting diplomas and certificates concerning your education and special vocational skills, as well as English and foreign language certificates. The USCIS requests these types of records because the more education and skills you have, the less likely you are to become a public burden. Take this request seriously and provide copies of records of all educational and vocational skills that you have, because the USCIS takes this seriously. All certificates must be accompanied by an English translation or an appropriate US evaluation document.

Additional miscellaneous evidence that the applicant is required to provide for the Form I-944, if applicable, are unemployment compensation records, pension records, foreign income records, retirement records, and child support records. Further, if you are unable to provide certain documents, you must provide notarized explanations of why these documents are not available.

Moreover, if one spouse does not meet the financial requirements, the other spouse, a friend, or a relative can act as a sponsor by filing a Form I-864 for an affidavit of support, together with the most recent tax transcript and tax return. To strengthen the application, the sponsor should include three years of tax documents, recent pay stubs, an employment verification letter, and evidence of assets. If a sponsor has a low income himself, but has substantial assets, he can still act as a sponsor.

Documents needed to prove family relations and financial ties

This is by far the most important selection of the documents that you must provide and the requirements that most applicants fail to satisfy. The USCIS routinely delays or denies green card applications because the couple fails to submit sufficient evidence to establish that family relations and financial ties exist between the spouses. Please note that some of these documents, such as joint tax transcripts, serve a dual role and help you to establish family ties, as well as income requirements.

Family photos

Take many photos of your family's activities, such as going out with friends and relatives, going on vacations, enjoying yourself outdoors, and attending entertainment events. You should submit all of these pictures to the USCIS with your application and keep a second set of pictures to yourself, so that you can refer to them during the interview and show them to the interviewing officer. You can write a description on each picture to indicate where and under what circumstances a particular picture was taken. You should submit at least 30 pictures from different events.

Joint checking account

You should establish at least one joint checking account and actively use it. You should have your payroll checks deposited to this account, pay bills from this account, and use the relevant ATM card to make purchases. When you submit your application, you should submit at least three months of bank statements with your application and bring three of the most recent statements to the interview as well. Aside from the primary checking account, try to establish a secondary joint checking account and a joint savings account and attach statements of these accounts as well.

Other financial accounts

Aside from the checking account, you can also establish a joint brokerage account or a joint IRA retirement account, or any type of financial account; alternatively, you may consider adding your spouse as a beneficiary to an existing account. For example, you can establish a joint brokerage account with www.etrade.com. Even if you do not believe in investing, you can invest in a conservative mutual fund, such as a municipal or corporate bond mutual fund or a utility fund. These types of funds fluctuate very little in price and pay out about 3-7% yearly dividends. An example of this kind of fund is PGIM Jennison Utility A (symbol PRUAX) and Northern Tax-exempt (Symbol NOTEX) mutual funds. I do not endorse these particular funds in any way. I merely give you an example. If a brokerage account sounds too complicated, you can open individual mutual funds accounts in both names. Some mutual funds only require a small initial investment of $100 to open an account. Although it is not required, having some additional financial accounts will give you extra points on financial family ties during the interview.

Joint credit cards or credit cards with the spouse as an authorized user

If you live as spouses, you are expected to have joint credit cards. You should attach at least three joint credit card statements or, if a second spouse is an authorized user, you can just make copies of your credit cards, showing that your cards have the same account number. If you do not have joint credit cards, you should open a new joint account, or have one spouse add the second spouse as an authorized user. If you do not have a good credit history, some banks, such as Discover or Citibank, at the time this book was written, were offering to open a secure credit card to people with no credit card history. Moreover, if you have a limited credit history, you can try applying for a card at CapitalOne Bank, Synchrony Bank, department stores, gas stations, and online catalogs, such as www.fingerhut.com. There are entire websites that sort credit cards by different criteria, such as a credit score, and some credit cards even offer substantial bonuses to new account holders, such as www.creditcards.com or www.hustlermoneyblog.com. The bottom line is that, even if you regard credit cards as evil, you should still have a few joint cards for the purpose of your green card application.

Joint utility bills

As spouses, you are also expected to have utility bills in both names. The utility and cable companies usually allow two names to be placed on the bill. If you only have one name on the bill, you should call your utility company and request that a second name be added. You should attach these joint utility bills to your green card application.

Joint insurance

You may also provide a joint insurance policy as proof of your family ties. Insurance of all kinds is counted, including medical, dental, property, life, car, renter, and coop and condo insurance. If you cannot obtain full medical and dental insurance, you may consider purchasing emergency medical insurance and a dental referral plan that charges pre-negotiated fees. Such plans are relatively inexpensive. Insuring property in your household is also inexpensive, but still counts as a point in your favor. In addition, you can obtain a life insurance policy for only one thousand dollars, which costs very little.

Affidavit of marriage relationship by the third party

You will also need an "affidavit of marriage relationship by the third party," which consist of letters from friends and relatives that know about your marriage and that describe your relationship, to the best of their knowledge. Preferably, you should get three such affidavits and have your friends or relatives to sign and to notarize the affidavit. In the letter, the contact information for your friends or relatives must be listed, such as phone number or e-mail address.

Driver's licenses with the same address

Some people move around a lot and forget to update the address on their driver's license. However, for the immigration petition, you should make sure that both of your driver's licenses have the same address.

IRS Transcripts and Joint Taxes

You will also need official IRS tax transcripts of your taxes, copies of your filed taxes, as well as W-2s and similar forms, preferably, for the last three years. You can request the tax transcripts by calling the IRS or from the IRS website. If you and your spouse filed separately, you will also need a second set of all the tax documents. The couple should try to avoid filing taxes separately because this will raise doubts about your family unity. Still, if all of your other evidence looks solid, the mere act of filing your taxes separately should not bar your green card application, but you should have an explanation for why you filed your taxes separately.

Miscellaneous evidence

You may submit other miscellaneous evidence of the family ties that, in your opinion, helps your application and demonstrates family relationships. For example, you can include tickets that have both names and were purchased for the same event. You can write an explanation on the copy of the tickets, such as that you traveled on the same airline to attend a certain event. Other examples include a joint gym membership, joint lease, joint invitation to a wedding, records of sending flowers, a company registered in both names, adoption records for a child, a child's school records showing both parents listed as emergency contacts, copies of conversations from social websites, conversations via text message, email exchanges, receipts for gifts, wills in which each spouse is a beneficiary of the other spouse, records showing one spouse as the beneficiary of the other spouse's retirement account, car insurance in both names, or an employment record showing that the other spouse is the emergency contact.

Possible issues to avoid

Certain situations may be treated as red flags and weaknesses in your application, and if this situation cannot be avoided you should prepare a good explanation of the problem area. Possible issues may include multiple previous immigration petitions of one of the spouses, a significant age difference between the spouses, spouses not residing together at the same address, spouses not speaking the same language, and the marriage taking place after the commencement of a USCIS deportation proceeding. You should be ready for these types of questions.

Work Permit and Travel Document

When filing for a marriage-based green card, you may also file for a work permit application (Form I-765) and a travel document application (Form I-131). The work-permit application has no separate fee, if it is submitted with the main application. Moreover, once you receive your employment authorization card, you may apply for a Social Security number from the Social Security Office, if no social security number has been issued to you previously. Simply take the employment document to your local Social Security Office and file an application for a Social Security number.

As for the travel document, there is a common misconception that you can use it to travel, just as you would use a regular green card. It may seem that you can use it to embark on a Caribbean vacation, and so on, but this is not the purpose of the travel document. Although there is no fee to apply for the travel document, if you apply for it with your main application, you must provide a reason for why you need to travel abroad, such as to visit a terminally ill family member. You are also required to provide supporting documents for your reason, such as a medical note indicating that this relative is terminally ill.

The USCIS states, in the instructions for the travel document application, that it has broad discretion not to allow the green card applicant back into the United States when he or she travels with a travel document. As such, you should think twice before traveling abroad with a travel document. My professional advice is to skip applying for the travel document and do not travel abroad until you are approved for the green card. Although some people claim that they routinely travel abroad with the travel document, I recommend that you not take that risk.

www.ingramcontent.com/pod-product-compliance
Lightning Source LLC
Chambersburg PA
CBHW050321220526
45465CB00005B/2073